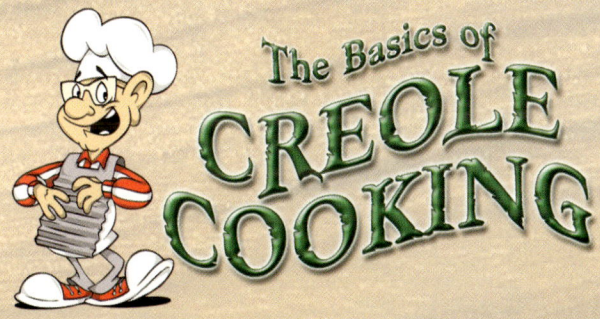

Published by: Tony Chachere's Creole Foods of Opelousas, Inc.
P.O. Box 1639, Opelousas, Louisiana 70571

Copyright 2002
Tony Chachere's Creole Foods of Opelousas, Inc.

Customer Service 1-800-551-9066
www.tonychachere.com

Second Edition

First Printing, September 2002

© 2002 by Tony Chachere's Creole Foods of Opelousas, Inc.

All rights reserved. This book or any part thereof may not be reproduced in any form without the written permission of Tony Chachere's Creole Foods of Opelousas, Inc.

Printed in Canada

Louisiana Legend

⁂ Tony Chachere ⁂
"The Ole Master"

Tony Chachere was one of the most colorful characters in Louisiana folk history. Born Anthony Chachere in 1905 in the little town of Opelousas, Louisiana, his parents were the descendants of French Creoles.

In 1972, Tony published Cajun Country Cookbook. His cookbook became known for its traditional Louisiana dishes, like gumbo, jambalaya and etouffée. Also included in the first edition was the recipe for his famous seasoning blend, Creole Seasoning, and he boasted that one recipe alone was "worth the price of the book". He sold 10,000 copies of his book in only one week.

Tony semi-retired from the operations of his food company in 1981 at the age of 76. He continued to perfect his recipes and to develop new food products. At this point in his life, his name became a household word in the Gulf South, synonymous with South Louisiana cooking. A glowing climax to his career in the culinary arts came in March 1995 when his colleagues in the American Culinary Federation honored him as the first inductee in the Louisiana Chefs' Hall of Fame. He died one week later, three months shy of his 90th birthday.

Getting Started

Basic Vegetable Mixture

1 onion
2 stalks celery
1/2 green bell pepper
1 clove garlic

Run vegetables through meat grinder or blender. You can double this recipe to suit your needs. Yields 1 cup.

Basic Cream Sauce

4 oz. margarine
2 tsp. all-purpose flour
1 pint Half-and-Half® cream

Melt margarine in a saucepan over medium heat. Add flour, stir well and add cream (slowly) while stirring. Continue stirring until you get a thick sauce. To this sauce, you can add mushrooms, shrimp, crab meat, grated cheese, white wine, lemon juice, egg yolks or any combination of these. Yields 2 cups.

Basic Brown Sauce
(for all meats and game)

Pan drippings
1 Tbsp. chopped green onions
1 Tbsp. parsley, minced
All-purpose flour (enough to thicken)

Use pan drippings (remove excess fat) of meat or game. To this add green onions, parsley and enough flour and water to thicken. Cook about 5 minutes. If desired, add mushrooms. If you like gravy on the sweet side, add 1 tablespoon currant jelly.

For a delicious Oil Free / Fat Free Roux try Tony Chachere's Instant Roux Mix.

Basic Red Sauce

1 stick margarine
1 (8 oz.) can tomato sauce
1/2 tsp. sugar
1 tsp. Worcestershire sauce
1 tsp. lemon juice
Tony Chachere's Original Creole Seasoning
2 cups Basic Vegetable Mixture
1 quart water

Melt margarine in heavy saucepan, add tomato sauce and sugar and cook 5 minutes. Add all other ingredients, including water. Simmer for 2 hours over low heat until thick. Add more water if needed and season to taste. Yields 4 cups.

For ITALIAN DISHES, add herbs and cheese.
For FISH DISHES, add mushrooms, shrimp or crab meat.

Basic Roux
(the basis for all stews and gumbos)

1 cup all-purpose flour
1 cup oil or margarine

Heat oil in heavy pot or Dutch oven. When oil is hot, gradually add flour, stirring continuously until well mixed. Lower heat and continue stirring until chocolate brown. When roux is chocolate brown, remove from pot and set aside. If roux remains in the pot, it will continue to cook and get too dark. Always use warm water to dissolve the roux. While you're at it, make more than enough as it keeps well in or out of the refrigerator.

• Roux •

Seafood Recipes

Barbecued Shrimp

1 lb. deheaded shrimp
1 stick margarine
Tony Chachere's Original Creole Seasoning

Place shrimp in flat pan. Slice margarine on top, then sprinkle all over with Tony Chachere's Original Creole Seasoning. Place in broiler and broil on one side until red. Then turn over and broil other side until red. (This takes very little time so be careful not to burn the shrimp). Mix well and use hot French bread to soak up the juice.

Shrimp Creole

1 onion, chopped
1/2 bell pepper, chopped
2 cloves garlic, chopped
1 rib celery, chopped
4 Tbsp. margarine
1 cup water
1 (8 oz.) can tomato sauce
1/2 tsp. thyme
1/2 tsp. crushed bay leaf
1/2 tsp. basil
1 lb. peeled shrimp
Tony Chachere's Original Creole Seasoning

In a Dutch oven, sauté vegetables in margarine for 5 minutes; add water, tomato sauce, thyme, bay leaf and basil. Cover and simmer for 45 minutes. Add shrimp seasoned with Tony Chachere's Original Creole Seasoning and cook covered for 30 minutes. If sauce is too thick, add water. Serve over steamed rice. Yields 4 servings.

Tony's Shrimp Etouffée

1 lb. peeled shrimp tails
Tony Chachere's Original Creole Seasoning
1 stick margarine
1 Tbsp. paprika
1 medium onion, chopped
1/2 bell pepper, chopped
2 cloves garlic, minced
2 cups water
1 Tbsp. Worcestershire sauce
2 Tbsp. corn starch
2 Tbsp. chopped green onions
Parsley

Season shrimp generously with Tony Chachere's Original Creole Seasoning. In an aluminum Dutch oven, melt margarine. Do not use an iron pot because it will cause shrimp to darken. Add paprika to margarine. Sauté shrimp about 5 minutes. Remove shrimp and set aside.

To pot add onions, bell pepper and garlic. Sauté until soft, about 10 minutes. Return shrimp to pot and add water and Worcestershire sauce. Stir and simmer slowly about 40 minutes. Check for taste, add more seasoning if necessary. Add mixture of corn starch and water slowly until slightly thickened. Serve with rice and garnish with green onions and parsley. Yields about 4 servings.

· Shrimp Creole ·

∞ Shrimp Salad ∞

1 lb. boiled shrimp, peeled, deveined and chopped
1 rib celery, finely chopped
1 hard-boiled egg, finely chopped
1 sweet pickle, finely chopped
1/2 tsp. minced capers
2 Tbsp. mayonnaise
Tony Chachere's Original Creole Seasoning

Place shrimp in a bowl. Add celery, egg, pickle, capers and mayonnaise. Mix thoroughly and add Tony Chachere's Original Creole Seasoning to taste. Serve on lettuce leaves or stuff into avocado or tomato halves. Yields 4 - 6 servings.

∞ Shrimp Boulets ∞

1 lb. shrimp, peeled and deveined
1 onion, finely chopped
1 bell pepper, finely chopped
2 sticks celery, finely chopped
2 cloves garlic, minced
1 Tbsp. paprika
2 eggs
1 cup bread crumbs
Tony Chachere's Original Creole Seasoning

Chop shrimp into about 4 pieces. Combine onion, bell pepper, celery, garlic, paprika, eggs and bread crumbs. Season with Tony Chachere's Original Creole Seasoning. If too dry, add water. If too soft, add bread crumbs. Roll in 1 1/2 inch balls or make patties. Dip in flour and fry in deep fat. Serve as hors d'oeuvres or use in shrimp bisque.

∞ Tony's Shrimp Stew ∞

1 lb. shrimp, peeled
Tony Chachere's Original Creole Seasoning
4 Tbsp. margarine
3 Tbsp. all-purpose flour
1 onion, chopped
1 bell pepper, chopped
2 ribs celery, chopped
1 clove garlic, minced
1 Tbsp. chopped green onions

Season shrimp with Tony Chachere's Original Creole Seasoning and refrigerate. Make a roux with margarine and flour in an aluminum Dutch oven. When chocolate colored, removed from heat and add all vegetables, except green onions. Stir mixture until it stops sizzling; add shrimp and enough warm water to cover all ingredients. Return to heat and simmer for 30 minutes. Serve over steamed rice and garnish with green onions. Yields 4 servings.

∞ Fried Shrimp ∞

1 lb. shrimp (26 - 30 count)
2 eggs
1 (5 oz.) can evaporated milk
1 Tbsp. baking powder
2 Tbsp. vinegar
Tony Chachere's Original Creole Seasoning
1 cup all-purpose flour
Oil for frying

Remove head and shell from shrimp, but leave fantail. Split shrimp down back and devein.

In a bowl, make a mixture of eggs, milk, baking powder and vinegar. Marinate shrimp for at least 1 hour in this mixture. Remove shrimp from mixture and season lightly with Tony Chachere's Original Creole Seasoning. Dip in flour and deep fry in 380° oil no longer than 1 1/2 minutes. Yields 3-4 servings.

For a special treat try Tony Chachere's Shredded Coconut Shrimp Batter when frying shrimp!

∞ Six Ways to Fry Fish ∞

1. Season fish generously with Tony Chachere's Original Creole Seasoning. In a paper bag, place 2 cups corn meal and 1 cup all-purpose flour. Make a slit lengthwise in perch or cut into bite-size pieces. Add to corn meal mixture in paper bag and shake. Remove from bag, shake off excess mixture and drop in oil (375°). Fry until brown and turn over once when they float. Remove and drain on absorbent paper.

2. For a change, spread mustard on fish before dipping in flour and corn meal mixture. Fry as directed above.

3. Soak in milk one hour. Drain, add to bag and shake. Remove and fry the same way.

4. Soak fish in beer for 10 minutes before placing in paper bag. Fry the same way.

5. Cut slit lengthwise in perch and place in dishpan. Season all over generously with Tony Chachere's Original Creole Seasoning, dash Worcestershire sauce and Louisiana Red Hot Sauce® (mix all over fish inside and out). Dip in mixture of 2 cups corn meal and 1 cup flour, then shake and fry in oil.

6. Instead of dipping in corn meal and flour, try pancake batter made by adding milk to soften. Dip seasoned fish and fry in oil.

∞ Baked Red Snapper ∞

1 (4 lb.) red snapper
Tony Chachere's Original Creole Seasoning
2 sticks margarine
1 (8 oz.) can tomato sauce
1 tsp. sugar
1 Tbsp. Worcestershire sauce
1 cup chopped onions
1 cup chopped celery
1/2 cup chopped green bell peppers
4 cloves garlic, minced
1/4 cup dry white wine

Season fish inside and out and place in open baking pan. Make a sauce with margarine, tomato sauce, sugar, Worcestershire sauce and vegetables. Cook over low heat for 1 hour. Pour wine over red snapper, followed by the sauce. Place in 300° oven and cook for 1 hour, basting occasionally. Serve with mashed potatoes. Yields 8 servings.

∞ Grilled Catfish Fillets ∞

Italian dressing
Mustard
Worcestershire sauce
2 (7 oz.) catfish fillets
Tony Chachere's Original Creole Seasoning

In a small bowl, mix Italian dressing, mustard and Worcestershire sauce. Rub on fillets. Sprinkle Tony Chachere's Original Creole Seasoning on fillets. Allow to marinate 1 hour in refrigerator. Use charcoal grill. Grill fillets 3 minutes on each side. Yields 2 servings.

• *Fried Seafood Platter* •

Fried Crawfish Tails

2 eggs
1 (5 oz.) can evaporated milk
1 Tbsp. baking powder
2 Tbsp. vinegar
1 lb. peeled crawfish tails
Tony Chachere's Original Creole Seasoning
1 cup all-purpose flour
Oil for frying

In a large bowl, mix eggs, milk, baking powder and vinegar. Season crawfish tails with Tony Chachere's Original Creole Seasoning and marinate in mixture at least 1 hour. Remove, dip each crawfish tail in flour and deep fry in 380° oil until golden brown. Yields 4 servings.

Crawfish Etouffée

4 Tbsp. margarine
1 lb. crawfish tails
Tony Chachere's Original Creole Seasoning
1 onion, chopped
1/2 bell pepper, chopped
2 cloves garlic, minced
1 tsp. corn starch
1 Tbsp. chopped green onions

Melt margarine in aluminum pot. Season crawfish tails generously with Tony Chachere's Original Creole Seasoning and sauté for 3 minutes. Remove crawfish tails and set aside. Add onions, bell pepper and garlic to the pot. Sauté 10 minutes. Return crawfish tails to pot; dissolve 1 teaspoon corn starch in 1 cup cold water and add. Stir and simmer slowly about 20 minutes. Adjust seasoning. Serve over steamed rice and garnish with green onions. Yields 4 servings.

Crawfish Stew

4 Tbsp. margarine
3 Tbsp. all-purpose flour
1 onion, chopped
1 bell pepper, chopped
1 clove garlic, chopped
2 ribs celery, chopped
1 lb. crawfish tails
Tony Chachere's Original Creole Seasoning
1 Tbsp. chopped green onions

Make a roux with margarine and flour in an aluminum pot. When chocolate colored, remove from heat and add vegetables. Stir mixture until it stops sizzling. Add crawfish, Tony Chachere's Original Creole Seasoning and water to cover all ingredients. Simmer 30 minutes. Serve over steamed rice and garnish with green onions. Yields 4 servings.

Crawfish Pie

1 lb. crawfish tails, peeled
1/2 stick margarine
2 cups Basic Vegetable Mixture
Tony Chachere's Original Creole Seasoning
1 (10 3/4 oz.) can cream of mushroom soup
1 unbaked pie shell and top

Sauté crawfish tails in margarine about 5 minutes. Remove crawfish tails, add Basic Vegetable Mixture to margarine and sauté for 10 minutes. Season crawfish and add to mixture, along with the soup. Cook at least 20 minutes. If too thick, add a little Sauterne wine or water. Place in pie shell and cover with top. Bake in 300° oven until brown. Yields 4 servings.

• Crawfish Etouffée •

Crawfish Bisque

4 level Tbsp. all-purpose flour
2 sticks margarine
1 onion, chopped
1 stalk celery, chopped
2 cloves garlic, minced
2 oz. tomato paste
1 Tbsp. Worcestershire sauce
1 tsp. sugar
1 lb. crawfish tails, peeled
2 quarts warm water
24 fried stuffed crawfish shells or boulettes
Tony Chachere's Original Creole Seasoning
1/4 lemon, sliced
1 Tbsp. chopped green onions
1 Tbsp. chopped parsley

Make a roux with flour and margarine in aluminum Dutch oven (do not use cast iron pot as this will cause crawfish to darken.) Remove from heat and add all chopped vegetables, except onion tops and parsley. Return to heat and stir until it stops sizzling. Add tomato paste, Worcestershire sauce, sugar and crawfish tails. Sauté for 5 minutes. Add 2 quarts warm water and bring to a boil. Reduce heat and simmer 1 hour. Add stuffed crawfish shells or crawfish boulettes and cook 30 minutes. Season with Tony Chachere's Original Creole Seasoning to taste.

Serve in soup bowls over steamed rice. Place 6 stuffed shells or 6 boulettes in each bowl. Garnish with lemon slices, green onions and parsley. Yields 4 servings.

Crawfish Fettuccine

2 onions, chopped
2 ribs celery, chopped
1 bell pepper, chopped
1 green onion, chopped
6 Tbsp. margarine
2 Tbsp. all-purpose flour
1/8 cup chopped parsley
2 lbs. crawfish tails
2 Tbsp. Jalapeño relish
1/2 lb. Velveeta cheese, cubed
1/2 pint Half and Half®
3 cloves garlic, minced
Tony Chachere's Original Creole Seasoning
1/2 lb. Fettuccine pasta
Cooking spray
1/2 cup Parmesan cheese

In a Dutch oven, sauté onions, celery, bell pepper and green onions in margarine on medium heat until tender. Add flour, parsley and crawfish and cook for 15 minutes. Add relish, cheese, Half and Half® and garlic. Reduce heat and simmer for 10 minutes. Stir often to prevent sticking. Season with Tony Chachere's Original Creole Seasoning.

During the last 10 minutes of cooking crawfish, begin boiling the pasta so that it will be tender at the same time that the crawfish is cooked. Follow directions on the bag to boil the pasta, but do not add salt. When the pasta is tender, drain, rinse in cold water and drain again.

In 1 or 2 casseroles coated with cooking spray, pour some of the pasta across evenly, then cover with crawfish mixture. Continue alternating pasta and crawfish mixture until all is used up. Sprinkle top with Parmesan cheese (optional). Bake at 350° for 15 minutes. Yields 8 servings.

• *Louisiana Crawfish* •

Crab Meat Dip

3 Tbsp. butter
1/2 cup all-purpose flour
1/8 tsp. prepared mustard
Tony Chachere's Original Creole Seasoning
3 cups milk
1/2 lb. shredded sharp Cheddar cheese
1 lb. lump crab meat

Melt butter in a double boiler. Stir in flour, mustard and Tony Chachere's Original Creole Seasoning. Blend well. Add milk to mixture gradually. Stir constantly until thickened. Add cheese, stirring until melted. Fold in crab meat and heat about 5 minutes, stirring occasionally. Pour into chafing dish. Yields 4 dozen small canape shells.

Mushrooms Stuffed with Crab Meat

8 large mushrooms
1 cup lump crab meat
1 Tbsp. bread crumbs
1 Tbsp. chopped onions
Tony Chachere's Original Creole Seasoning
2 Tbsp. chopped parsley
1 egg, slightly beaten
Bread crumbs
Parmesan cheese

Rinse mushrooms and remove stems. In a bowl, mix crab meat with bread crumbs, onion, Tony Chachere's Original Creole Seasoning and parsley. Add egg and mix well. Fill mushroom caps with mixture and sprinkle with bread crumbs and cheese. Place in 350° oven until light brown. Yields 8 mushrooms.

Corn & Crab Meat Bisque

4 Tbsp. butter
3 Tbsp. all-purpose flour
1 large onion, finely chopped
1 (15 oz.) can cream-style corn
1 (10 3/4 oz.) can cream of potato soup
1 quart Half and Half®
1/2 tsp. mace
1 lb. lump crab meat
1/2 lb. shredded Swiss cheese
1 Tbsp. chopped parsley
1 Tbsp. chopped green onions
1 Tbsp. dry sherry
Tony Chachere's Original Creole Seasoning

In a 3-quart pot, melt butter and add flour to make a blond roux. Sauté onions until tender; add corn, soup, Half and Half®, mace and crab meat. Bring to a boil, then reduce heat. Add cheese, parsley, green onions and sherry. Season with Tony Chachere's Original Creole Seasoning. Remove from heat and serve. Yields 12 servings.

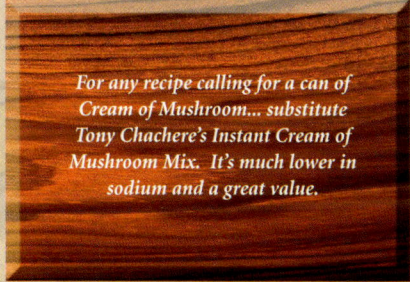

For any recipe calling for a can of Cream of Mushroom... substitute Tony Chachere's Instant Cream of Mushroom Mix. It's much lower in sodium and a great value.

• Corn & Crab Meat Bisque •

◦ Crab Meat Au Gratin ◦

8 Tbsp. margarine
1 onion, chopped
2 ribs celery, chopped
4 Tbsp. all-purpose flour
1 (12 oz.) can evaporated milk
1 (15 oz.) can evaporated milk
2 egg yolks
2 lbs. lump crab meat
Tony Chachere's Original Creole Seasoning
1 cup shredded Cheddar cheese
Cooking spray

Melt margarine in skillet; sauté onions and celery until tender. Add flour and blend well; add milk. Cook over low heat until thick, stirring constantly. Remove from heat; add egg yolks, crab meat, Tony Chachere's Original Creole Seasoning and half of cheese. Transfer to square casserole coated with cooking spray and top with remaining cheese. Bake at 350° for 20 minutes. Yields 6 servings.

◦ Louisiana Crab Cakes ◦

2 eggs
2 Tbsp. mayonnaise
1 tsp. Creole mustard
1/3 cup minced onions
1 lb. claw crab meat
Tony Chachere's Original Creole Seasoning
1 cup bread crumbs
Oil for frying

In a large bowl, blend together eggs, mayonnaise, mustard and onions. Beat well. Fold in crab meat, then add Tony Chachere's Original Creole Seasoning. Mix well. Using a tablespoon, dip out a large spoonful. Form into a round cake, then coat each side with bread crumbs. In a heavy skillet, heat oil to 350°. Fry each crab cake until golden brown. Remove and drain on absorbent paper. Yields 8 cakes.

• *Louisiana Blue Point Crab* •

∽ Crab Stew ∽

4 Tbsp. margarine
4 Tbsp. all-purpose flour
1 onion, minced
1/2 bell pepper, chopped
1 (14 1/2 oz.) can stewed tomatoes
2 cloves garlic, minced
2 sprigs parsley, chopped
2 green onions, chopped
Tony Chachere's Original Creole Seasoning
12 medium crabs, cleaned

In a Dutch oven, melt margarine and stir in flour to make a brown roux. Add onions and bell pepper. When onions have become transparent, add other ingredients. Season with Tony Chachere's Original Creole Seasoning. Cook about 30 minutes on low heat. Add crabs. Cook in gravy for 30 minutes. If gravy becomes too thick, add water to desired consistency. Serve over steamed rice. Yields 4 servings.

∽ Fried Oysters ∽

1 quart oysters
2 eggs, beaten
1/4 cup milk
Tony Chachere's Original Creole Seasoning
2 cups all-purpose flour
2 cups corn meal

Drain oysters and set aside. In one bowl, combine eggs, milk and seasoning. In a separate bowl, combine flour and corn meal. Roll oysters in flour mixture. Dip in egg mixture, then again in flour mixture. Deep fry in 375° oil until golden brown. Yields 6 servings.

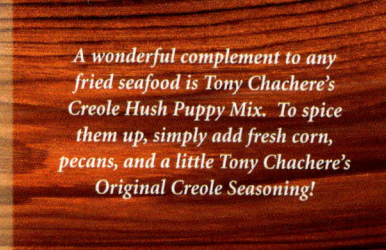

A wonderful complement to any fried seafood is Tony Chachere's Creole Hush Puppy Mix. To spice them up, simply add fresh corn, pecans, and a little Tony Chachere's Original Creole Seasoning!

∽ Oysters Bienville ∽

1 stick butter or margarine
4 Tbsp. all-purpose flour
1 pint Half and Half®
1 (4 oz.) can mushrooms
1/2 cup chopped boiled shrimp
1/2 cup chopped parsley
1/2 cup chopped onions
1/2 tsp. thyme
1/4 cup grated Parmesan cheese
1/4 cup dry white wine
6 egg yolks
36 oysters
Tony Chachere's Original Creole Seasoning
6 large pastry shells, baked

Melt butter in a Dutch oven. Add flour; stir for 2 minutes. Add cream and stir until thick. Add all other ingredients except egg yolks and oysters. Stir well until cheese is melted. Do not overheat. Remove from heat and slowly add beaten egg yolks, stirring constantly. Heat oysters in their own liquor in a saucepan until edges begin to curl. Pour off liquor and reserve. Stir oysters into mixture and cook 5 minutes. Add oyster liquor if too thick. Season with Tony Chachere's Original Creole Seasoning. Place 6 oysters in each pastry shell. Place shells in a shallow baking pan and fill each shell with sauce. Bake in 400° oven about 10 minutes. Serve immediately. Yields 6 servings.

∽ Oysters en Brochette ∽

6 slices bacon
3 dozen select oysters
Tony Chachere's Original Creole Seasoning
1 cup bread crumbs
1 stick margarine, melted
6 skewers, 6 inches long

Cut bacon in pieces same length as oysters. Alternate pieces of bacon and oysters on skewer, 6 on each. Season to taste. Dip filled skewer in bread crumbs, then in melted margarine. Broil or cook over hot coals 5 to 10 minutes until bacon is crisp. Serve with toast and Tartar Sauce. Yields 3 servings. *Scallops or clams may be used instead of oysters.*

Cajun/Creole Classics

Red Beans & Rice

1 lb. dried red beans, soaked overnight
1/2 lb. pickled pork, cut in strips
1 onion, finely chopped
1/2 green bell pepper, chopped
Tony Chachere's Original Creole Seasoning

Combine all ingredients with enough water to cover well and cook until beans are tender. Add water from time to time to make a thick, rich gravy. Serve with steamed rice. Yields 6 servings.

Chicken & Okra Gumbo

1 (4 to 6 lb.) hen, cut into pieces
Tony Chachere's Original Creole Seasoning
4 Tbsp. oil
2 cups chopped fresh okra
1 stick margarine
4 Tbsp. flour
1 Tbsp. Worcestershire sauce
1 large onion, chopped
2 stalks celery, chopped
1 green bell pepper, chopped
4 cloves garlic, minced
3 quarts water
3 Tbsp. chopped green onions

Season chicken with Tony Chachere's Original Creole Seasoning. In a large aluminum Dutch oven, fry seasoned chicken in 2 tablespoons oil until brown. Remove and set aside. Add 2 more tablespoons oil and fry chopped okra for about 10 minutes, stirring constantly to keep from burning. Add a roux made with margarine and flour. Add chicken, Worcestershire sauce, chopped onion, celery, bell pepper, garlic and water. Bring to a boil and simmer 2 to 3 hours or until meat is tender. Skim off excess fat and serve in soup bowls with rice. Garnish with chopped green onions. Yields 10 servings.

Isabell's Creole Pork Roast

1 (5 lb.) pork roast
Tony Chachere's Original Creole Seasoning
1 cup basic vegetable mixture

Make 10 slits in roast. Add 1 tablespoon of Tony Chachere's Original Creole Seasoning to vegetable mixture; stuff mixture into slits equally. Rub seasoning all over roast.

Place roast in Dutch oven. Cook in a 350° oven until roast is brown. Cover, reduce heat to 300° and cook for 3 hours or until roast is tender. You may thicken the gravy with a mixture of water and flour. Skim off excess fat. Yields 10 servings.

Chicken & Sausage Jambalaya

1 (3 lb.) fryer, cut up
Tony Chachere's Original Creole Seasoning
4 Tbsp. margarine
4 onions, chopped
4 cloves garlic, minced
2 ribs celery, chopped
1 bell pepper, chopped
1/2 lb. smoked pork sausage
3 cups uncooked rice
6 cups water

Season chicken generously with Tony Chachere's Original Creole Seasoning. Add margarine to a 5-quart Dutch oven and fry chicken until brown. Remove chicken from pot and add all vegetables. Sauté for 10 minutes. Add sausage and rice and cook for 10 minutes, mixing thoroughly. Return chicken to pot; add water and stir. Cover and simmer about 30 minutes or until rice is fully cooked. Yields 8 servings.

Tony Chachere's offers an entire line of truly authentic Cajun/Creole dishes, produced in the Cajun Heartland of Louisiana. From Jambalaya and Gumbo to Red Beans & Rice, we create your favorites!

Old-Fashioned Chicken Stew

1 (6 lb.) hen, cut up
1 Tbsp. shortening
2 Tbsp. all-purpose flour
3 onions, finely chopped
4 cups warm water
Tony Chachere's Original Creole Seasoning
1/4 cup chopped green onions and parsley

In a Dutch oven, brown chicken in shortening; remove from pot. Place flour in pot and stir until brown. Add onions and cook until tender. Add chicken and water. Season with Tony Chachere's Original Creole Seasoning. Simmer until tender (about 1 hour). During the last 5 minutes of cooking, add green onions and parsley. Stir occasionally as stew thickens to prevent burning. Serve over steamed rice. Yields 6 servings.

Cajun Rolled Steak

1 large round steak
Tony Chachere's Original Creole Seasoning
1 onion, sliced
1 bell pepper, sliced
3 ribs celery, chopped
String or toothpicks
1 Tbsp. oil

Season round steak with Tony Chachere's Original Creole Seasoning. Spread onion, bell pepper and celery evenly on steak. Roll up jelly style and tie with string or secure with toothpicks. Place in a skillet with oil. Cook on medium heat until brown, adding a little water while cooking. Steak will make its own gravy. Cover and cook for 45 minutes or until tender. Adjust seasoning. Slice and serve over steamed rice. Yields 6 servings.

Delicious Shrimp & Corn Soup

1/4 cup oil
1/4 cup all-purpose flour
1 onion, chopped
3 cloves garlic, chopped
1 bell pepper, chopped
2 ribs celery, chopped
2 (14 1/4 oz.) cans stewed tomatoes
1 (15 oz.) can cream-style corn
1 (16 oz.) bag frozen corn
1 gallon water
2 lbs. shrimp, peeled
Tony Chachere's Original Creole Seasoning

In a large pot, make a light roux by stirring oil into flour over medium heat. Remove from heat and add onion, garlic, bell pepper and celery. Cook until sizzling ceases. Return to medium heat. Add tomatoes; cook 10 minutes, stirring constantly. Add corn and water. Reduce heat and simmer 1 hour. Bring to a boil and add shrimp; cook 20 minutes. Season with Tony Chachere's Original Creole Seasoning and serve. Yields 12 servings.

• Shrimp & Corn Soup •

Creole Vegetable Soup

2 lbs. heavy beef brisket or soup bone
3 quarts water
Tony Chachere's Original Creole Seasoning
2 ribs celery
1 large onion
1 large Irish potato
1 (20 oz.) can tomatoes
1 cup chopped cabbage
3 carrots, chopped
2 stalks celery, chopped
1/2 onion, chopped
1/2 potato, chopped
2 sprigs parsley, minced
1 (15 oz.) can whole kernel corn
1 turnip, diced
2 Tbsp. uncooked rice
Small amount broken spaghetti or macaroni

In a 4-quart covered pot, boil meat in seasoned water with whole ribs of celery, whole onion and whole potato. Simmer for 3 hours or longer. Take soup meat from pot and remove meat from bone. Chop into bite-size pieces, discarding bone and fat.

Mash well-cooked vegetables through a strainer. Return these ingredients and meat to the liquid. Add all other vegetables and rice; cook until vegetables are well done. Break small amount of spaghetti or macaroni into soup during last 20 minutes of cooking. Yields 10 servings.

Dirty Rice has always been a great side dish for any occasion. To save a little time and money, try Tony Chachere's Dirty Rice Mix. It also works great as a stuffing for baked turkey and boneless chickens!

Stuffed Cabbage Rolls

1 medium head firm cabbage
1 lb. ground beef
1/4 lb. ground ham
1 cup cooked rice
1 egg, well beaten
1 onion, finely chopped
1/2 cup milk
Tony Chachere's Original Creole Seasoning
Toothpicks
1/2 cup water
1 cup Basic Red Sauce

Clean cabbage and remove core. Steam or boil until leaves are wilted and pliable. Separate leaves and reserve 8 to 10 of the largest for rolls.

Thoroughly mix beef, ham, rice, egg, onion, milk and seasoning. Fill each leaf separately with mixture. Wrap leaf securely, envelope-fashion, and skewer with toothpicks.

Place flat down in Dutch oven or heavy saucepan. Add water and Basic Red Sauce and place remaining leaves on top. Cover tightly and cook over low heat for 1 1/2 hours. Add small amount of water if necessary. Yields 8-10 servings.

Dirty Rice

1 lb. chicken giblets
1 lb. ground beef
1 cup chopped onions
1/2 cup chopped bell pepper
1/2 cup chopped celery with leaves
1/4 cup chopped parsley
Juice of 2 crushed garlic cloves
Tony Chachere's Original Creole Seasoning
1/4 cup chopped green onions
Pinch thyme and basil
2 cups rice

In a pot, boil giblets in salt water until tender; reserve liquid. In a Dutch oven, sauté meat until brown. Drain off excess fat, add remaining ingredients, and continue to cook a few minutes. In a separate pot, cook rice in 4 cups of giblet liquid for 18 minutes. Drain rice and mix thoroughly into the meat mixture. Spoon into a greased casserole and bake at 300° for 20 to 30 minutes or until dry. Yields 10 servings.

All-Time Favorites

Tony's Meat Balls and Spaghetti

1/2 lb. lean ground pork
1/2 lb. lean ground beef
1/2 cup crushed crackers
1 Tbsp. chopped parsley
1/2 cup chopped green onions
1/4 cup grated Romano cheese
Tony Chachere's Original Creole Seasoning
3 eggs, well beaten
1 cup milk
1 cup olive oil

To make meat balls, in a large bowl combine all ingredients, except milk and oil. Add enough milk to make soft mixture. Wet hands with water and roll into 16 very soft meat balls (add milk to mixture if not soft enough). The trick to tender meat balls is to fill them with air rather than compacting them into a ball. Place meat ball in hand cupped upward and gently toss the ball upward a few times to fill with air. Fry in oil in a heavy Dutch oven until brown. Remove from pot and set aside.

sauce

1 onion, chopped
2 cloves garlic, minced
1/2 bell pepper, chopped
2 (6 oz.) cans tomato paste
1 Tbsp. sugar
1 fresh basil leaf
10 or more anise seeds to taste
1 quart water
Tony Chachere's Original Creole Seasoning

To the same Dutch oven add onion, garlic and bell pepper. Sauté until tender. Add tomato paste; cook 10 minutes. Add sugar, basil, anise and water. Simmer for 1 hour. Add meat balls and cook slowly for an additional hour. Adjust seasoning. Skim off excess fat. Pour over spaghetti and serve. Yields 8 servings.

Potato Salad

5 lbs. potatoes
8 eggs
1/2 cup mayonnaise
3 Tbsp. Creole mustard
Tony Chachere's Original Creole Seasoning
Paprika

Peel potatoes and cut into large chunks. In a large pot, boil eggs and potatoes for 20 minutes (a little longer if potatoes are still hard). Place potatoes in a large bowl. Peel eggs and extract the yolks. In another bowl, mash yolks and mix with mayonnaise and mustard until creamy. Chop egg whites and place in the bowl with potatoes. Add yolk mixture and blend well. Season with Tony Chachere's Original Creole Seasoning. Serve immediately or chill and serve cold. Garnish with sprinkle of paprika. Yields 10 servings.

Bloody Mary

1 oz. vodka
4 oz. tomato juice
Dash of Worcestershire sauce
Dash of hot pepper sauce
Dash of celery salt
Dash of lemon juice
Tony Chachere's Original Creole Seasoning

Combine all ingredients and shake in a cocktail shaker. Rim glass with Tony Chachere's Original Creole Seasoning; fill glass with ice and pour mixture into glass. Garnish with celery, pickled okra or pickled string bean. Yields 1 serving.

Bloody Mary

❀ Old-Fashioned Creole Corn Bread ❀

2 cups yellow corn meal
1 cup all-purpose flour
1 cup sour cream
3 tsp. baking powder
1/2 cup sugar
2 eggs
1 cup cream-style corn
1 1/2 tsp. salt
1/2 cup bacon drippings
Milk

In a large bowl, mix all ingredients together, except milk; stir until well blended. Add enough milk to make the mixture pour easily. Spoon into greased muffin tins or baking pan. Bake in 400° oven for 20 to 30 minutes or until golden brown. Yields 8 servings.

❀ Opelousas Baked Chicken ❀

4 fryer halves
Tony Chachere's Original Creole Seasoning
1 cup leftover chicken fat or oil
1 cup water
4 Tbsp. paprika

Season chicken generously with Tony Chachere's Original Creole Seasoning. Rub well on each side and place in open baking pan. Cover with a mixture of the oil and water and place pan in oven at 275° and bake until hot. Sprinkle generously with paprika and baste continuously about every half hour until dark, dark brown. The cooking period will be about 3 to 5 hours. Yields 4 servings.

This is a very famous Opelousas dish. The secret is in the seasoning and the long, slow basting process. It's served with rice dressing, petit pois, candied yams, green salad, French bread and black coffee demi-tasse.

For the most flavorful and juiciest chicken you've ever tasted... inject it with one of Tony Chachere's Creole Injectable Marinades before cooking.

❀ Maque Chou ❀

12 ears tender fresh corn
4 Tbsp. margarine
1 onion, chopped
1 bell pepper, chopped
1 clove garlic, minced
1 tomato, diced
Tony Chachere's Original Creole Seasoning
1 cup milk

In a large bowl, cut corn off cob and scrape cobs to get all the juice; set aside. Heat margarine in a Dutch oven; add onion, bell pepper and garlic. Sauté until tender. Add corn, tomato and Tony Chachere's Original Creole Seasoning. Cook mixture over medium heat for 1 hour, stirring often. Add a little milk from time to time to keep mixture soft. Yields 12 servings as a side dish.

❀ Tony's He-Man Chili ❀

1 lb. hot sausage (Louisiana or Italian)
1 lb. lean ground beef
1 onion, chopped
1 bell pepper, chopped
2 cloves garlic, minced
1 Louisiana hot green pepper or Jalapeño, diced
1 cup Burgundy wine
1 tsp. dry mustard
1 tsp. celery seeds
2 Tbsp. chili powder
3 cups chopped Roma tomatoes
Tony Chachere's Original Creole Seasoning
1 (15 1/2 oz.) can pinto beans
2 (15 1/2 oz.) cans kidney beans

Slice sausage into 1-inch pieces and fry in a Dutch oven until brown. Remove and set aside. Pour off excess fat and fry ground beef. Drain and set aside with sausage. Pour excess fat from pot. Cook onions, bell pepper, garlic and hot pepper over low heat until tender. Stir in wine, mustard, celery seeds and chili powder. Simmer 10 minutes. In a bowl, mash tomatoes; pour into pot. Add meats. Bring to a boil. Reduce heat; season with Tony Chachere's Original Creole Seasoning. Simmer for 30 minutes, stirring occasionally. Add beans and their liquid; return to a boil. Reduce heat and simmer for 1 hour, stirring occasionally. Yields 12 servings.

Fried Okra

24 okra pods (4 inches or shorter)
Tony Chachere's Original Creole Seasoning
1 egg, beaten
Cracker crumbs
Oil for frying

Wash okra, drain. Season with Tony Chachere's Original Creole Seasoning. Roll the pods in the egg, then in cracker crumbs. Deep fry in hot oil until delicate brown. Drain on absorbent paper and serve as hot as possible. Yields 4 servings.

Seafood Gumbo

1 cup all-purpose flour
1 cup oil
2 cups chopped okra
4 Tbsp. margarine
1 cup chopped onions
1/2 cup chopped celery
1/2 cup chopped bell pepper
4 cloves garlic, minced
1 (14 1/2 oz.) can stewed tomatoes
3 quarts warm water
Tony Chachere's Original Creole Seasoning
4 gumbo crabs, cut in half
2 lbs. peeled shrimp, deveined
1/2 pint oysters
1/2 cup finely chopped green onions and parsley
Filé

In a skillet, make a dark roux with flour and oil. Remove from heat and set aside. In a large aluminum Dutch oven or stock pot, sauté okra in margarine until it is no longer stringy. Add onions, celery, bell pepper and garlic and sauté until tender. Add roux, tomatoes and water to this mixture and season with Tony Chachere's Original Creole Seasoning. Simmer for 1 hour. Add seafood and simmer for 30 minutes. Serve in soup bowls over steamed rice and garnish with green onions, parsley and a dash of filé. Yields 8 servings.

Harold's Hand Salad

2 heads lettuce
2 bunches parsley
2 bunches green onions
4 Roma tomatoes or 3 cups ripe cherry tomatoes
2 cups small round radishes
1 (6 oz.) can ripe black olives
1 (2 oz.) jar stuffed olives with pimiento
2 (6 1/2 oz.) jars artichoke hearts
1 (10 oz.) bottle pickled cauliflower
12 Italian pickled peppers
Tony Chachere's Original Creole Seasoning
1 (8 oz.) bottle Italian salad dressing

Wash vegetables in cold water and drain. Break lettuce into bite-size pieces. Chop parsley and cut green onions in 3-inch pieces. Dice tomatoes and cut radishes in half. Drain and discard juice of olives, artichokes, cauliflower and peppers. Put all ingredients in a large salad bowl. Season with Tony Chachere's Original Creole Seasoning to taste; add salad dressing (enough to barely coat) and toss. Yields 12 servings.

Smothered Okra & Tomatoes

2 lbs. okra
3 Tbsp. oil
1 Tbsp. all-purpose flour
1 onion, chopped
1/2 bell pepper, chopped
2 ribs celery, chopped
5 tomatoes, chopped
Tony Chachere's Original Creole Seasoning

Wash okra. Cut in 1/8 inch slices. Fry in an aluminum pot on medium heat in 2 tablespoons oil until okra is no longer sticky.

In another skillet, make a medium dark roux with 1 tablespoon oil and flour. Add onion, bell pepper and celery. Simmer until tender. Add tomatoes and simmer for 5 minutes. Add okra, seasoned with Tony Chachere's Original Creole Seasoning. Simmer for 1 hour. Yields 6 servings.

Banana Nut Bread

1 stick margarine
1 cup sugar
2 large ripe bananas, well mashed
1 Tbsp. baking soda
2 Tbsp. hot water
2 eggs, slightly beaten
1 tsp. lemon juice
1/2 cup chopped nuts
2 cups all-purpose flour

Cream sugar and margarine until light and fluffy in a medium-size mixing bowl. Add bananas. Place baking soda in hot water until dissolved and add to mixture. Add eggs, lemon juice, nuts and flour to creamed mixture. Stir just enough to combine ingredients. Pour batter into wax paper-lined loaf pan. Bake at 350° for 1 hour. Remove bread from pan and peel off paper. Serve warm or cold. Yields 12 servings.

Black-Eyed Peas

1 lb. black-eyed peas
3 quarts water
1 cup chopped onions
1 bell pepper, chopped
1/2 cup chopped parsley
2 bay leaves
1 tsp. basil
Tony Chachere's Original Creole Seasoning
Ham bone
1 lb. smoked sausage, cut in 1/2 inch slices

In a medium pot, soak peas overnight in enough water to cover. Drain and rinse. Place all ingredients, except the sausage, in a heavy pot and cook for 1 hour. Meanwhile, brown the sausage in a skillet and drain. Add sausage to the beans and continue cooking until creamy. Add a little oil for creaminess when lean ham or pork is used.

Any kind of pork may be substituted for the sausage, including ham, salt meat, pickled pork, or andouille. Black-eyed peas are usually served over rice. However, a soup may be made of black-eyed peas, red beans, or white beans. Yields 6 servings.

Broccoli Casserole

1 large onion, chopped
1/2 stick margarine
3 (10 oz.) packages chopped broccoli
2 cups cream of mushroom soup
1 1/2 rolls garlic cheese
1 (4 oz.) can mushrooms
1/2 cup chopped blanched almonds
Tony Chachere's Original Creole Seasoning
1/2 cup bread crumbs

In a medium-size saucepan, sauté onions in margarine. When onions are wilted, add drained broccoli, mushroom soup, cheese, mushrooms and 1/4 cup almonds. Cook until cheese is completely melted. Season with Tony Chachere's Original Creole Seasoning and pour into a casserole. Sprinkle with almonds and bread crumbs and bake at 300° until bubbly. Yields 8 servings.

Baked Potato Soup

4 potatoes
4 Tbsp. margarine
2/3 cup all-purpose flour
6 cups milk
Tony Chachere's Original Creole Seasoning
4 green onions, chopped
12 slices bacon, cooked, crumbled
1 1/4 cups shredded Cheddar cheese
1 (8 oz.) carton sour cream

Wash potatoes and prick several times with a fork; bake at 400° for 1 hour or until cooked. Let cool. Cut potatoes in half lengthwise; scoop out pulp and set aside in a bowl. Discard skins. Melt margarine in a heavy saucepan over low heat; add flour, stirring until smooth. Cook 1 minute, stirring constantly. Gradually add milk; cook over medium heat, stirring constantly, until mixture is thickened and bubbly. Add potato pulp, Tony Chachere's Original Creole Seasoning, 2 tablespoons green onions, 1/2 cup bacon and 1 cup cheese. Cook until thoroughly heated. Stir in sour cream. Add extra milk, if necessary, for desired consistency. Serve with remaining green onions, bacon, and cheese. Yields 12 servings.

Southern Chicken Pie

5 Tbsp. margarine
1 onion, chopped
4 Tbsp. all-purpose flour
2 cups chicken broth
Tony Chachere's Original Creole Seasoning
2 1/2 cups cooked chicken pieces
2 cups diced ham
1 large can biscuit dough

Melt margarine over low heat in a heavy pan; add onions and cook until transparent. Add flour and stir until blended. Slowly add chicken broth and stir over low heat until thick and smooth. Season with Tony Chachere's Original Creole Seasoning. Arrange chicken meat in layers with diced ham in a large casserole, or in 6 ramekins. Cover with sauce. Top with biscuit dough, toasted bread crumbs, or pastry. Bake in 350° oven for 20 minutes. Yields 6 servings.

Creamed Onions

12 small white onions
6 Tbsp. margarine
8 level Tbsp. flour
2 cups milk
1/2 lb. cheddar cheese, grated
Tony Chachere's Original Creole Seasoning
Paprika

In salted water, boil onions until fork-tender. In a medium-size saucepan, melt margarine over low heat, add flour and stir until well blended. Remove from heat, gradually stir in milk and return to heat. Cook, stirring constantly, until thick and smooth. Add onions, cheese and seasoning. To serve, sprinkle with paprika. Yields 4 servings.

Pecan Pie

3 eggs
1/2 cup sugar
1 cup white or dark Karo syrup
1 tsp. vanilla extract
1 cup chopped pecans
1/2 tsp. salt
1 (9-inch) unbaked pie shell

In a small saucepan, beat eggs slightly and add sugar, Karo, vanilla, nuts and salt. Beat well after each addition. Pour into unbaked 9-inch pie shell and bake at 325° for 50 minutes or until brown. For miniature pies, place pie dough in muffin pan, fill with mixture and bake same as above. Yields 1 pie or about 8 servings.

Tony's Baked Picnic Ham

1 (8 lb.) picnic ham (deboned)
1 Tbsp. whole cloves
1/2 lb. brown sugar
1 Tbsp. yellow mustard
1 (8 oz.) can crushed pineapple
1 pint jar pitted cherries

In a medium-size saucepan, boil ham for one hour. Remove and slice off skin. Using a sharp knife, score with diamond-shape cuts. Stud with whole cloves.

Place ham in open pan and bake for one hour. While ham is baking, make a glaze using pineapple juice, mustard and brown sugar. Cook slowly until sauce thickens.

Once ham has baked one hour, spoon glaze evenly. Cover with crushed pineapple and decorate with cherries. Cook for an additional thirty minutes. Slice and serve. Yields 10-12 servings.

To get that sweet professional praline taste out of every bite of your picnic ham, inject it with Tony Chachere's Praline Honey Ham Injectable Marinade. It's sure to be a hit with everyone!

Wild Game Recipes

Wild Duck A La George

4 whole ducks, dressed
Tony Chachere's Original Creole Seasoning
4 onions
4 stalks celery
1 bell pepper
1 cup bacon drippings
1 cup Burgundy wine
2 (10 1/2 oz.) cans chicken broth
1 cup chopped, mixed green onions and parsley
1 (8 oz.) can mushrooms

Season ducks inside and out generously with Tony Chachere's Original Creole Seasoning. Chop vegetables, mix and add equally to inside of each duck.

Place ducks in black Dutch oven on top of stove, add bacon drippings and brown ducks all over. Add wine, chicken broth and enough water to cover ducks. Bring to a boil. Reduce heat to simmer and cook until tender. Remove from pot and add green onions, parsley, mushrooms and mushroom juice thickened with a little flour. Cook 5 minutes. Add water if more gravy is needed. It takes 3 to 4 hours to completely cook. Yields 8 servings.

• Wild Duck A La George •

Roasted Rabbit

1 rabbit, dressed
Tony Chachere's Original Creole Seasoning
1 cup bread crumbs
1/2 cup ground pork
1/2 cup ground beef
1 egg, slightly beaten
1 Tbsp. all-purpose flour
1 onion, chopped
1 carrot, chopped
1 sprig parsley, chopped
1 sprig thyme, crushed
1 bay leaf, crushed
4 cloves garlic
1 cup hot water
1 cup milk
1 stick margarine, melted
1/2 cup white wine
Currant jelly

Wash rabbit and soak in slightly salted water for 1 hour or more. Dry and rub well with Tony Chachere's Original Creole Seasoning. Stuff with a dressing prepared from the bread crumbs, ground meat mixed with egg and seasoning. Skewer together, sift flour over rabbit and place in roasting pan on a bed of chopped onion, carrot, parsley, crushed thyme, bay leaf and cloves. Moisten with hot water. Cover and roast in 300° oven, basting frequently for 2 hours. Baste with milk the first hour then use the melted margarine. Before serving, add wine to gravy and pour over rabbit. Serve with wine and currant jelly. Yields 4 servings.

Wild Duck, Sausage & Oyster Gumbo

1 cup all-purpose flour
1 cup oil
4 onions, chopped
4 stalks celery, chopped
1 bell pepper, chopped
1/2 cup chopped parsley
1 lb. andouille or sausage, cut in 1/2 inch slices
4 wild ducks, cut into pieces
1 pint water
Tony Chachere's Original Creole Seasoning
1 bay leaf
3 pints oysters
Green onions, chopped
Filé

Make a roux with the flour and oil. Then add onions, celery, bell pepper and parsley and cook until tender. Add duck pieces and sausage and cook until meat is browned. Add water. Next add Tony Chachere's Original Creole Seasoning and bay leaf. Cover and let simmer for 1 1/2 to 2 hours or until ducks are tender. Add oysters and oyster liquid. Uncover and cook for 20 minutes. Serve over rice with a sprinkle of green onions and filé. Serves about 8 to 9 people.

Tony's Barbecued Alligator Tail

Cut tail into one-inch thick slices like steak. Season generously with Tony Chachere's Original Creole Seasoning. Place on a pit and dab with a mixture of 1 pint barbecue sauce and 1 stick margarine. Serve with the sauce. It's great! Yields 6 servings.

Opelousas Baked Duck

1 (5 to 7 lb.) duck, cut in half
Tony Chachere's Original Creole Seasoning
4 Tbsp. paprika
1 cup oil
1 cup water

Season duck halves generously with Tony Chachere's Original Creole Seasoning. Sprinkle, skin side up, with paprika and place in an open baking pan.

Over the halves, pour a mixture of oil and water. Bake at 275° for 3 to 5 hours, basting every half hour. Remove duck halves, pour off excess fat and save for next cooking. Yields 4 servings.

Long, slow cooking, along with the basting, is the secret. Of course, the seasoning has everything to do with the taste. Pan drippings can also be used in rice dressing.

Tony's Quail Recipe

1 stick butter or margarine
Tony Chachere's Original Creole Seasoning
6 quail
1 Tbsp. chopped onions
1 Tbsp. chopped celery
1 Tbsp. chopped green bell pepper
1 cup chicken broth
1 Tbsp. sherry wine
1 strip bacon, chopped
1 (4 oz.) can mushrooms
1 Tbsp. flour
1 Tbsp. currant jelly

In a Dutch oven, melt butter. Season quail with Tony Chachere's Original Creole Seasoning and fry until brown. Remove birds and stuff each cavity with vegetable mixture. Replace in pot and add broth, wine and bacon. Cover, place in 300° oven and cook 1 hour until tender. Remove quail, add mushrooms and a little flour to thicken. One tablespoon currant jelly goes well in the gravy. Yields 6 servings.

❦ Roast Venison ❦

Hind quarter of venison (about 10 pounds)
Tony Chachere's Original Creole Seasoning
2 sticks margarine, sliced
1 green bell pepper, chopped
1 onion, chopped
2 stalks celery, chopped
4 cloves garlic, minced
1 cup burgundy wine
4 strips bacon
1 Tbsp. all-purpose flour
1 (8 oz.) can mushrooms
1 Tbsp. minced green onions
1 Tbsp. minced parsley

Cut a pocket along the leg bone from the large end almost to small end. Season the roast well inside pocket and rub well outside. Fill pocket with margarine and all the chopped vegetables, except green onions, parsley and mushrooms. Pour wine over roast and place 4 strips bacon on top.

Place in covered roasting pan and cook in 300° oven for 3 to 4 hours until tender. Remove from pan, add tablespoon of flour to juice from mushrooms and mix well. Add mushrooms, green onions and parsley to pan juices. Place over high heat and cook 5 minutes until gravy thickens. Put roast back into gravy and cook uncovered for 5 minutes to brown. If you like your gravy sweet, add 2 tablespoons currant jelly. Slice and serve 1/2 pound per person. Yields 16 servings.

❦ Tony's Venison Chops ❦

4 large venison shoulder chops
Tony Chachere's Original Creole Seasoning
2 Tbsp. vegetable oil
1 cup honey
1 cup dry white wine
2 Tbsp. Worcestershire sauce
1 large clove garlic, crushed
1/2 tsp. powdered ginger
Few drops of Tabasco® sauce

Season and brown chops slowly on both sides in oil. Combine remaining ingredients, mix well, pour over chops. Simmer over very low heat about 45 minutes or until tender. Serve chops and sauce over hot, buttered pasta. Yields 4 servings.

❦ Cajun Squirrel Stew ❦

4 squirrels, cut in pieces, including the heads
Tony Chachere's Original Creole Seasoning
1 stick margarine
1 cup chopped onions
1/2 cup chopped green bell peppers
4 cloves garlic, chopped
1 Tbsp. Worcestershire sauce
1/2 cup Burgundy wine
1 Tbsp. all-purpose flour
1 (4 oz.) can mushrooms
1 Tbsp. chopped green onions
1 Tbsp. chopped parsley

Cut each squirrel into eight pieces, including the heads. Season with Tony Chachere's Original Creole Seasoning. Melt margarine in a Dutch oven and fry squirrels until browned all over and starting to stick to the pot. Add onions, bell peppers and garlic and cook 5 minutes.

When vegetables are soft, add a small amount of cold water and a tablespoon of Worcestershire sauce and cover the pot. Let simmer about 1 hour. Stir well and add 1/2 cup burgundy wine. Cook until squirrels are tender.

Remove the squirrels from the pot and to the remaining juices add flour mixed with liquid from the can of mushrooms. Add a mixture of green onions, parsley and mushrooms. Cook for 5 minutes and stir until slightly thickened. Pour over squirrels. Serve over steamed rice. Yields 8 servings.

• Roast Venison •

❦ Smothered Doves Acadienne ❦

2 sticks margarine
8 doves, cleaned
Tony Chachere's Original Creole Seasoning
2 onions, chopped
2 stalks celery, chopped
1 bell pepper, chopped
4 cloves garlic, finely chopped
1 Tbsp. Worcestershire sauce
1 cup Burgundy wine
1 (4 oz.) can mushrooms
1 Tbsp. all-purpose flour
1 Tbsp. chopped parsley
2 Tbsp. chopped green onions

Melt margarine in Dutch oven, add doves seasoned with Tony Chachere's Original Creole Seasoning and cook until brown. Stir constantly until they begin to stick to the bottom. Add onions, celery, bell pepper, garlic and Worcestershire sauce. Cook until wilted. Add Burgundy, cover and simmer 2 to 3 hours or until birds are tender. *As you know, doves are tough and need a long time to cook.* Add 4 ounces cold water if needed.

When doves are tender, remove from the pan liquid. Add mushrooms, mixture of flour blended with the mushroom juice, green onions and parsley. If you like a sweet gravy, add 2 tablespoons currant jelly. Serve with spaghetti or steamed rice. Yields 8 servings.

❦ Venison Parmesan ❦

1 lb. thin venison steak (1/4 inch thick)
Tony Chachere's Original Creole Seasoning
1 egg
2 tsp. water
1/3 cup grated Parmesan cheese
1/3 cup fine dried bread crumbs
1/4 cup olive oil
1 onion, finely chopped
2 Tbsp. butter
1 (6 oz.) can tomato paste
2 cups hot water
1/2 tsp. marjoram
1/2 lb. Mozzarella or Swiss cheese

Cut steaks into 6 or 8 pieces, sprinkle with Tony Chachere's Original Creole Seasoning. Beat egg with 2 teaspoons water. Dip meat in egg, then roll in mixture of Parmesan cheese and bread crumbs. Heat oil in large skillet and fry the pieces (about 3 at a time) until golden brown on each side. Lay in shallow, wide baking dish.

In the same skillet, sauté onion in butter until soft. Add tomato paste mixed with hot water, Tony Chachere's Original Creole Seasoning and marjoram. Boil a few minutes, scraping all of the brown bits from the bottom. Pour most of the sauce over steaks and top with thin slices of cheese. Pour remaining sauce over steaks and bake at 350° for about 30 minutes. Yields 4 servings.

Tony Chachere's Marinade Recipes

⚘ Deep Fried Turkey ⚘

1 whole turkey (thawed completely)
Tony Chachere's Injectable Marinade
Tony Chachere's Original Creole Seasoning

Rinse turkey with warm water. Remove giblets and rinse again. Drain cavity well.

Inject turkey with the following amounts at the points indicated on the illustration. (Use the injection technique described on the label of Tony Chachere's Injectable Marinade package)

Points A: Inject a FULL injector into each breast.
Points B: Inject a FULL injector into each thigh.
Points C: Inject 1/2 oz. into each drumstick.

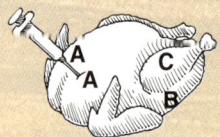

When injecting, redirect needle in different directions through the same hole to maximize marinade coverage at points indicated in the illustration.

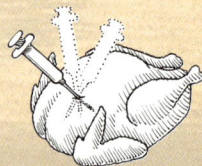

Sprinkle inside and outside of turkey generously with Tony Chachere's Original Creole Seasoning.

Deep Fry: Be sure to drain all water from turkey cavity before deep-frying to prevent splattering of hot oil. Deep-fry whole turkey in 3-4 gallons of oil at 325°F for 3-1/2 minutes per pound (whole chickens for 7 minutes per pound).

You may also bake in a conventional manner.

⚘ Grilled Chicken ⚘ Quarters

4 chicken quarters
Tony Chachere's Injectable Marinade
  (the flavor of your choice will do just fine)
Tony Chachere's Original Creole Seasoning

Inject each chicken quarter as per the directions on the package of Tony Chachere's Injectable Marinade. Generously season the outside of the chicken quarters with Tony Chachere's Original Creole Seasoning. Grill each side on medium heat for about 15 minutes or until the meat temperature reaches 180 degrees.

⚘ Tony Chachere's ⚘ "Best Burgers in Town"

2 lbs. ground chuck
1/2 cup Tony Chachere's Injectable Marinade
  (we suggest Honey Bacon BBQ)
1/2 tsp. Tony Chachere's Original Creole Seasoning

In a large mixing bowl, combine all ingredients. Shape 1/4 lb. of meat mixture into burgers. Grill or pan fry to medium well. Yields 8 juicy burgers.

∞ Spicy Shrimp ∞
Pasta Salad

1 (12 oz.) package ritini pasta, cooked & drained
1/2 red onion, sliced thinly
1 (2.25 oz.) can sliced black olives, drained
1 red bell pepper, sliced
1 lb. cooked salad shrimp
3 oz. crumbled feta cheese
Tony Chachere's Butter & Jalapeno Marinade

In a large salad bowl, toss all ingredients together. Cover and refrigerate over night. Yields 8 servings.

∞ Tony Chachere's ∞
Chicken Tenders

1 1/2 lbs. chicken breast strips
1/2 cup Tony Chachere's Butter & Jalapeno Marinade
1 (9 oz.) package Tony Chachere's Seasoned Fish Fry

Marinate chicken strips in Butter & Jalapeno marinade 4 hours to overnight. Dredge each piece in fish fry. Shake off excess and deep fry until golden brown. Yields 4-6 servings.

∞ Roasted ∞
Garlic & Herb
Pulled Pork Poboys

1 trimmed, boneless pork butt roast
Tony Chachere's Roasted Garlic & Herb Injectable Marinade
Tony Chachere's Original Creole Seasoning
Poboy French Bread
Mayonaise
Mustard
Grilled onions

Prepare roast by injecting meat with 1 - 1.5 oz. marinade per pound of total weight. Place in roasting pan. Season outside of roast generously with seasoning. Cover. Bake at 350° for approximately 30 minutes per pound. Remove from oven and let rest for 30 minutes. Slice roast and return to drippings. Keep warm in oven until ready to serve. Serve on Poboy bread and top with mayonaise, mustard, and grilled onions.

∞ Baked Praline ∞
Candied Yams

2 (23oz.) cans sweet potatoes, drained
1 1/2 cups Tony Chachere's Praline Honey Ham Injectable Marinade
1/3 cup golden raisins
1/2 cup chopped pecans
dash of cinnamon
3 Tbsp. butter

Preheat oven to 375°. In a baking dish, combine all ingredients. Cover. Bake for 35 minutes or until bubbly. Serve warm. Yields 8 servings.

• Deep Fried Turkey •

Tony's Southern Pecan Smoked Prime Rib

1 Rib roast (4 lbs. and up)
1 (17 oz.) Tony Chachere's Roasted Garlic & Herb Injectable Marinade
2 cups pecan pieces
Tony Chachere's Original Creole Seasoning
1/2 cup honey

Inject 1 - 2 oz. of Roasted Garlic & Herb marinade per pound of meat throughout. Rub roast generously with Tony Chachere's Original Creole Seasoning. Cover and place in oven. Cook at 350° until internal temperature reaches 100° (check with meat thermometer). Remove from oven. Pour honey over roast. Sprinkle pecans all over top of roast. Place back in oven until internal temperature reaches 120° (for rare), 140° (medium), or 160° (well done). Let cool 10 minutes and cut into 1 inch steaks and serve.

Honey Praline Ham

1 (10 lb.) Bone-in Ham
Tony Chachere's Praline Honey Ham Injectable Marinade
1 cup pecan pieces
1 cup brown sugar

Inject ham with Tony Chachere's Praline Honey Ham marinade. Score the top of the ham. Pour additional Praline Honey Ham Marinade over top of the ham. Rub brown sugar and pecans on top of ham. Place in a 300° oven for 1 hour. Let stand 10 minutes and serve.

Butter Jalapeno Fried Cornish Hen

1 Cornish Hen
Tony Chachere's Butter & Jalapeno Injectable Marinade
Tony Chachere's Original Creole Seasoning

Inject 3 oz. of Butter & Jalapeno marinade into cornish hen per instructions on marinade bottle. Cover with Tony Chachere's Original Creole Seasoning inside and out. Deep fry in 350° oil for approximately 12-15 minutes. Let cool 5-10 minutes and serve.

Roasted Garlic Brisket with Honey Bacon

1 (10 - 15 lb.) brisket
1 (17 oz.) Tony Chachere's Roasted Garlic & Herb Injectable Marinade
1 (17 oz.) Tony Chachere's Honey Bacon BBQ Injectable Marinade
Tony Chachere's Original Creole Seasoning

Place brisket fat side up in roasting pan. Inject 8 oz. Roasted Garlic & Herb Marinade all over brisket. Next, pour 8 oz. of Honey Bacon BBQ Marinade over brisket. Season brisket liberally with Tony Chachere's Original Creole Seasoning. Cover with foil and bake for 3 hours at 350°. Remove foil and bake an additional 45 minutes. Let cool for 10 minutes then serve.

Oven Roasted Honey Bacon BBQ Ribs

1 rack of St. Louis style ribs
Tony Chachere's Original Creole Seasoning
1 (17 oz.) Tony Chachere's Honey Bacon BBQ Injectable Marinade
1 1/2 cups water

Turn oven to broil. Place rib rack in roasting pan meat side up. Season to taste with seasoning. Broil until brown. Turn meat side down. Add marinade and water. Cover. Bake 2 1/2 hours or until tender at 375° F. Uncover. Bake an additional 10-15 minutes or until brown and caramelized.

Moist-N-Juicy Baked Chicken

1 (3 lb.) whole fryer
Tony Chachere's Original Creole Seasoning
1 (17 oz.) Tony Chachere's Creole Butter Injectable Marinade

Preheat oven to 400 F. Remove giblets from fryer and wash well. Place fryer in roasting pan. Inject marinade evenly throughout the chicken (about 1 oz. per pound). Season outside of fryer generously with seasoning. Cover. Bake for 2 1/2 hours or until chicken reaches an internal temperature of 170° F. Remove cover. Continue to bake approximately 10-15 minutes or until skin is brown and crispy.

∽ Butter Bacon ∽
Fried Dove

10 doves
1 (17 oz.) Tony Chachere's Butter Bacon Injectable Marinade
Tony Chachere's Original Creole Seasoning
1 cup milk
1 egg
2 cups pancake flour
Oil for frying

Clean doves, singe, split down the back and flatten. Inject 1 oz. of Tony Chachere's Butter Bacon Injectable Marinade into each breast. Season with Tony Chachere's Original Creole Seasoning. In a bowl, soak in mixture of milk and egg. When ready to fry, dip in pancake flour and deep fry in 375° oil. When doves float to the top, remove and drain on absorbent paper. The secret of tender doves is quick frying. Yields 5 servings.

∽ Grilled Quail ∽

16 quail, dressed
16 Jalapeño peppers
16 slices bacon
1 (8 oz.) bottle Italian salad dressing
1/2 cup Chablis
1/3 cup soy sauce
1/4 cup lemon juice
Tony Chachere's Original Creole Seasoning
1 (17 oz.) Tony Chachere's Creole Butter Injectable Marinade
Banana peppers, optional

Rinse quail thoroughly with water; pat dry. Place a Jalapeño pepper into body cavity of each quail. Wrap 1 bacon slice around each quail and secure with a toothpick. Place quail in a large shallow dish. In a bowl, combine Italian dressing and the next 4 ingredients; pour over quail. Inject 1 oz. Tony Chachere's Creole Butter Injectable Marinade into each quail. Cover and marinate in refrigerator overnight.

Remove quail from dish, reserving marinade. Prepare charcoal fire in one end of grill; burn 15-20 minutes, or until flames disappear and coals are white. Grill quail, covered, on opposite end for 1 hour, turning once, and basting often with marinade. Garnish with banana peppers, if desired. Yields 8 servings.

∽ Louisiana ∽
Meat Loaf

1 cup bread crumbs
1/2 cup red wine
1 lb. ground beef
1/2 lb. lean pork
3 Tbsp. chopped onions
3 Tbsp. finely chopped celery leaves
3 Tbsp. minced parsley
Tony Chachere's Original Creole Seasoning
1 (17 oz.) Tony Chachere's Honey Bacon BBQ Injectable Marinade

In a large bowl, moisten bread crumbs thoroughly with red wine. Add next six ingredients to bread mixture. Mold into a loaf (kneading with fingers is best). Place in a greased pan and cover with Tony Chachere's Honey Bacon BBQ Injectable Marinade. Bake in a 325° oven for 1 hour and 15 minutes, basting frequently. Do not allow to dry out. Add marinade when needed. Remove from oven, turn onto platter and slice. Yields 8 servings.

∽ Stuffed Turkey Breast ∽

2 onions, chopped
1 bell pepper, chopped
3 cloves garlic, minced
4 Tbsp. margarine
1/3 lb. tasso, cubed
1/2 cup bread crumbs
Tony Chachere's Original Creole Seasoning
2 boneless turkey breast halves
Cotton string
1 (17 oz.) Tony Chachere's Creole Butter Injectable Marinade

In a skillet, sauté onions, bell pepper, and garlic in margarine until tender. Add tasso and simmer 45 minutes, adding water as needed. Remove from heat and add bread crumbs and Tony Chachere's Original Creole Seasoning. Refrigerate 1 hour. To open each breast, cut a slit lengthwise so that they open completely. Stuff each half with the chilled mixture and roll. Secure by tying with string in three places. Inject 1 1/2 oz. of Tony Chachere's Creole Butter Injectable Marinade all over turkey breasts. Bake at 400° for 1 hour and 15 minutes. Slice into 3/4 inch thick slices. Yields 20 slices.

Dessert Recipes

Apple Pecan Cake

3 eggs
2 cups sugar
1 cup oil
2 tsp. vanilla extract
2 3/4 cups all-purpose flour
1 tsp. baking soda
1 tsp. salt
2 tsp. cinnamon
4 cups peeled, chopped apples
1 cup chopped pecans

In a large mixing bowl, beat eggs at medium speed with an electric mixer until thick and pale. Gradually add sugar, beating until blended. Add oil and vanilla; beat at low speed until blended. In a separate bowl, combine flour, baking soda, salt and cinnamon; add to egg mixture, stirring until blended. Stir in apples and pecans. Pour batter into a greased and floured 10-inch tube pan. Bake at 350° for 1 hour and 25 minutes or until a toothpick inserted in the center comes out clean. Cool cake in pan on a wire rack for 5 minutes; remove from pan and cool completely on wire rack. Yields 12 servings.

Chocolate Oatmeal Candy

1 1/2 cups sugar
1/2 cup brown sugar
4 Tbsp. cocoa
1/2 cup milk
1/4 cup butter, softened
1/2 cup peanut butter
3 cups oats
1/2 tsp. salt
1 tsp. vanilla extract

In a large saucepan, mix together sugars, cocoa, milk and butter. Stir over medium heat until well blended. Bring to a boil and cook for 2 minutes. Remove from heat. Add peanut butter and stir until smooth. Add oats, salt and vanilla. Mix thoroughly. Drop by tablespoonful onto waxed paper or cookie sheet and cool. Yields 24 pieces.

Opelousas Pralines

2 cups sugar
Pinch of salt
1 (5 oz.) can evaporated milk
2 Tbsp. sugar (heaping)
2 tsp. vanilla extract
3 cups shelled pecans

In a large saucepan, combine sugar, salt and milk. Cook to softball stage (test by dropping a little in water or use candy thermometer). Remove from heat.

While this is cooking, caramelize sugar (until brown) in a small, thick skillet. Combine with above mixture until it reaches test stage and remove from heat. Add vanilla and pecans and beat. Before candy crystallizes, dip out by separate spoonfuls and place on waxed paper to cool.

If mixture should crystallize too soon (before removing from saucepan), add a tablespoon of boiling water and beat again. Yields 24 pralines.

Peanut Brittle

3 cups sugar
1/2 cup water
3 cups raw peanuts
1 1/2 cups white corn syrup
3 tsp. baking soda

In a heavy saucepan, boil all of the ingredients, except soda, until nuts crack in syrup and syrup turns yellow. Remove from heat and add soda. Stir rapidly and pour onto greased cookie sheets. When cool (about 1 hour), break into serving-size pieces. Yields about 24 pieces.

· Opelousas Pralines ·

Notes

Notes